1140

Starving to Win: Athletes and Eating Disorders

Starving to Win: Athletes and Eating Disorders

Eileen O'Brien

The Rosen Publishing Group/New York

The Teen Health
Library of
Eating Disorder
Prevention

√**RAP** 435-7747

Acknowledgments: Information, help, and encouragement from many sources allowed me to write this book. Thank you Michele Drohan, Mary K. Duginske, Cherie Faison, Doug Fireside, Phil Hoose, Colleen Pierre, R.D., Glenwood Thomas, Laura Weeldreyer, and librarians of the Enoch Pratt Free Library's Central and Light Street branches! You're all wonderful!

The people pictured in this book are only models. They in no way practice or endorse the activities illustrated. Captions serve only to explain the subjects of photographs and do not in any way imply a connection between the real-life models and the staged situations. News agency photos are exceptions.

Published in 1998 by the Rosen Publishing Group, Inc.
29 East 21st Street, New York, NY 10010

Copyright © 1998 by the Rosen Publishing Group, Inc.

First Edition

Library of Congress Cataloging-in-Publication Data

O'Brien, Eileen, 1955–
    Starving to win : athletes and eating disorders / by Eileen O'Brien.
    p.cm. — (The teen health library of eating disorder prevention)
    Includes bibliographical references and index.
    Summary: Explains why many young athletes are vulnerable to eating disorders and what they can do to prevent them.
    ISBN: 0-8239-2764-4
    1. Eating disorders—Psychological aspects—juvenile literature. 2. Athletes—Diseases—Nutritional aspects—Juvenile literature. 3. Athletes—Nutrition—Juvenile literature. 4. Body image—Juvenile literature. [1. Eating disorders. 2. Athletes. 3. Body image.] I. Title. II. Series.
RC552.E18027 1998
616.85'26'0088796—dc21
                                          98-16884
                                            CIP
                                            AC

Manufactured in the United States of America

Contents

Introduction

Gina has been taking ballet lessons since she was five years old. Until this year, she always enjoyed her classes and looked forward to performing in the dance academy's annual recitals. Now, though, Gina moves through her lessons with a blank expression instead of her usual smile, and she hates going onstage. Last summer, just before entering eighth grade, Gina suddenly grew four inches taller. She is taller than her dance teacher and wears clothes a size larger than her own mother's—a fact her mother has repeated to all her friends. Her family and friends kid Gina, calling her "Big Bird" in school and at the dance academy, where she's taller than all of her classmates.

But Gina doesn't want to stand out; she wants to fit in. She's so worried about the prospect of growing even taller that she's uncomfortable eating. Most evenings, Gina takes her dinner up to her room, telling her parents that she needs to start her homework. Upstairs, she wraps pieces of her food in little wads of tissue and flushes them down the toilet.

Mr. McCarthy has coached girls' track at Nikki's high school for many years, and the team has brought home regional trophies nearly every year. Mr. M has always paired off older members of the team with new members in a "buddy system." He likes to say that the older buddies' job is to "turn babies into winners," but he's never given the girls on the team any special instructions for doing this.

When Nikki joined the track team, her assigned "buddy" was an intense, competitive junior named Kara. Kara has told Nikki to keep a list of everything she eats. Kara reviews this list at least once a week, writing down the number of calories next to each food on the list. After the first week she said desserts and snack foods were "off limits" until Nikki "earns" them by improving her practice times. Kara imposes the same discipline on herself, but with even higher goals: She doesn't allow herself any snacks unless she sets a personal record or wins an event.

By the end of her first season, Nikki is keeping her own food lists. She decides every week which foods to skip until she meets a goal in training or in other areas of her life. She is proud of her ability to stick to her plans. She even enjoys feeling a bit hungry, because to her it's proof of her determination and strong character.

Theo, a varsity wrestler, competes in the 156-to-160 weight class. He's always "made weight" at the weigh-ins held on the morning of every wrestling meet day. However, if his weight goes over 160, he'll have to sit out his match. He's heard from his teammates that the best way to avoid this is to skip breakfast and take an over-the-counter drug that "cleans out your system" first thing in the morning. They also told him to run laps around the gym until it's his turn to be weighed. Theo has never had to resort to doing this, but he has a package of laxative pills at home and has already made up his mind to take some if the bathroom scale reads 161 or higher on a meet day.

What Gina, Nikki, and Theo are doing to improve as athletes won't help their performances and could seriously hurt their bodies. Many teen athletes, anxious and unsure about the relationship between food, weight, and performance, make unhealthy eating choices. Too often, these athletes have extremely limited diets and weight-loss "secrets," which become patterns of deprivation that they cannot stop without help.

The eating disorders anorexia nervosa and bulimia nervosa are the most extreme examples of these patterns. Anorexia is self-starvation, and bulimia is a repeated cycle of overeating (bingeing), then getting the food out of the body before it can be digested (purging). These disorders are not fads, bad habits, or ways of expressing personality. They are illnesses that require treatment until the body recovers and the symptoms go away.

Many young athletes, including some outstanding performers, have ended their sports careers and hurt their bodies with severe dieting, fasting, purging, and other measures. Often, they do this in the hopes of improving their performance or impressing others. In recent years, the news media have reported the deaths of a nationally ranked female gymnast, a young ballet company member, and a college wrestler from illnesses and injuries that began with disordered approaches to food and exercise. Many other, less famous people have also lost their lives to eating disorders.

This book explains what eating disorders are and why people with disorders need help. It is not a substitute for treatment, which doctors and psychologists provide. You can read this book to prepare for discussions about food and health with a friend, family member, or trusted adult. But do not try to treat yourself or anyone else you think has an eating disorder.

Whatever your reason for wanting to know more about athletes and eating disorders, reading this book will give you information to make decisions and find support to help you play hard and live well.

Whose Body Is It?

Gina, the dancer who's suddenly taller than her classmates, has collected books about dancers since first grade. Most were gifts from her parents, grandparents, and friends who admired her ambition to become a ballet dancer. She has read, over and over, about the years of daily practice and the sacrifices of money, time, and fun that dancers make to become professionals. Women dancers in the corps de ballet perform their identical motions in beautiful matching costumes, wearing identical expressions on their faces. In an entire corps there seems to be no one who's a head taller than all the others, as Gina is now.

Convinced that no ballet company will want her, Gina feels like a failure at thirteen. She stopped looking through her dance books because they depress her. Although she's eating as little as possible and sticking to her daily practice routine, Gina is afraid that all her efforts won't matter if she gets much bigger. She thinks, I'll never be a dancer. My parents got me all my lessons and costumes and came to all my recitals for nothing! My friends will think I was just goofing around with dancing. They'll know I was never any good at it.

Gina does not share her thoughts with anybody. She's sure her friends, even her parents, won't respect her if she admits how she really feels about her future in ballet. For the same reasons, she continues to practice and take lessons. She has no idea whether skipping dinners will actually keep her from growing taller, but she does not know what else to try, and she is losing weight.

After a couple of weeks without eating a single dinner, Gina realizes with pleasure that she can do something. She can sit in front of a plate full of chicken and rice or other foods she's always liked and tell herself it's not good for her. As she breaks up the food with her fork so she can flush it away, she feels relief that she's winning this secret game. If she keeps it up, maybe she can have a ballerina's body.

The "Right" Type of Body

Athletes and performers are not the only people who can feel anxious about whether their bodies are the "right" type. Teenagers, especially girls, watch themselves very closely and worry that they're being watched and judged all the time. Unfortunately, there are real reasons to feel as if people are watching. Sometimes it seems as if everybody, from disk jockeys to the boys at school, has something to say about the "right" kind of female body, face, and fashion.

Commercials, magazine articles, music videos, and billboards focus on women's bodies. Television cameras zoom in while sports announcers scrutinize every play and player. In some

Many young women and men worry about not having the "ideal" kind of body commonly portrayed in the advertisements and photo spreads of most fashion magazines.

In sports like track and cross-country running, the clock determines who wins rather than the judges' votes.

sports, even the uniforms and hairdos are rated! And instructors' or coaches' ideas about the "right" kind of body for dancing, swimming, cheerleading, or basketball can be almost impossible to ignore. After all, aren't they the experts? With all these messages, it's hard to remember that other people's opinions are not the only determining factor in your success or happiness. In sports such as track and swimming, the clock picks the winners. These athletes work on improving their speed. The only question is: Who finished fastest? In team sports,

13

points are awarded for getting a ball through a net, goal, or fence that are the same for all players. They work on their scoring and defense skills. But gymnasts and figure skaters win competitions with votes from the judges. It's easy to see how an athlete competing for the judges' favor can focus his or her training on copying the body or the diet of a top-ranked star.

Some sports fans admire stars for their "victory" over food or fat as much as for their skills and style. When skaters are praised for following the same sugar-free diet for several years, or football players are admired for eating twenty hot dogs in one sitting, their athletic ability is connected to their eating habits. This connection makes self-starvation or binge-purge cycles seem almost normal for athletes.

Who's on Your Team?

Theo's high school wrestling team has gone to the state finals five of the last six years, and his coach was just named "Coach of the Year." Every season begins with a weigh-in and body-fat analysis of each player. And the results—actual weight and recommended "fighting weight"—are reported for each person at a team meeting. A few of the bigger wrestlers with the highest body-fat percentages are assigned fighting weights four to ten pounds below their actual weight.

The coach doesn't say, "You can't get on the bus if you're above your fighting weight." He doesn't have to.

Theo knows that if he gains more than five pounds during the season, he'll be benched. The coach shows a film every year about the dangers of taking steroids and other performance-boosting drugs, but he doesn't tell his wrestlers about the dangers of unhealthy eating habits and weight-loss practices.

Many coaches and trainers give advice about nutrition and meal planning to student athletes, especially in major sports like football. But other coaches may not have the time or knowledge to give their athletes more than vague encouragement to "keep up your strength" and "do what you have to to feel your best."

But students who aren't taught how to follow a training or high-performance diet may experiment with unhealthy habits. They may pick up bits of nutrition advice from infomercials, older students, and magazines. Or they may simply try to achieve the things their coaches praise most—competitive intensity, desire, or perfectionism—by taking one or two food guidelines to hurtful extremes. A gymnast whose coach tells her to "lighten up on the pasta," for example, might respond by cutting all carbohydrates out of her diet, eating only fruits and vegetables.

A coach can have a winning record, superior knowledge of the sport's rules and strategies, and great motivating skills, yet not know a lot about "eating to win." In most states a person does not need to take a nutrition class to become a physical education teacher or a coach. (However, many coaches and trainers do have up-to-date knowledge about nutrition, and many schools teach nutrition in health classes.) One survey of exercise instructors found that most of them had wrong information about the power of food and exercise to change a person's body. Just as important, a coach may not recognize that an athlete is losing weight because of an eating disorder.

Pleasing Your Coach

Disordered eating or exercising may begin as an effort to please a coach by an athlete. This person may willingly, even secretly, follow harsh self-imposed rules. In Michigan, a college wrestler died after working out for hours in a rubber suit that kept his overheated, dehydrated body from cooling off. According to teammates, he was attempting to "sweat out" and "burn off" twelve pounds in one day to make his weight.

Lisa Ervin was a teenage figure skater who moved away from her parents to live near her coach and prepare for Olympic competition. *Inside Edge*, a book about competitive figure skating, tells about an episode during Lisa's training when she gained a few pounds and her spins and jumps became a little

Some teens develop unhealthy eating and exercise habits in order to please a demanding coach.

weaker. When her coach pointed this out, Lisa volunteered for weekly weigh-ins, secretly fasting before each one and bingeing afterward.

She also punished herself for poor practice sessions with long workouts on an exercise bike. Lisa did not develop a full-blown eating disorder. But many young athletes who begin similar routines for a quick weight loss soon have an unbreakable habit and an eating disorder.

Body Basics

2

Nikki became an aunt for the first time last summer. She was thrilled when her older sister Vanessa and Vanessa's husband, Dwight, brought baby Eve to Nikki's house. The whole family crowded around the baby, waiting for their turn to hold her. Everyone tried to predict what this little baby would look like when she grew up.

"Look at that little pointy chin and those long fingers. She's going to take after her father."

"I hope she doesn't get Dwight's ears."

Nikki's mother took out an old photo. "This is Vanessa when I brought her home from the hospital!" she announced. "You can see that Eve is the image of her mother." When it was Nikki's turn to hold the baby, she pinched one of Eve's chubby cheeks and thought, I hope she doesn't get big thighs, like me.

The predictions made by Nikki and her relatives about Eve probably sound familiar. We expect babies to "take after" one or both parents. That makes sense, because each of us is born with a unique genetic heritage. This mix of biological traits is inherited from our mothers and fathers and built into all our cells.

Genetics and Body Shape

When babies grow into girls and boys and then women and men, why do so many people suddenly expect their bodies to have a "right" size and shape unrelated to family traits? Doesn't it make sense that your bone structure and metabolic rate (the speed at which your body uses food for energy) is influenced by genetics, as much as the curl of your hair and the color of your eyes?

It does make sense, and medical research has confirmed that it's true. Genetics matters more than diet, exercise, or any other single factor in the shape and size of our bodies. Scientists who studied a group

Genetics play a major role in determining the size and shape of your body when you grow up.

of adopted babies throughout their lives found that in size and weight, they were more like their birth parents than their adoptive parents. Similar results were found for sets of identical twins who were separated and raised in different families. With nothing in common except their genes, they grew up with virtually identical weights and body builds. So it's not entirely true that "you are what you eat."

All Bodies Need Fuel

But if you're an athlete, should you eat like one? Do you need more or different foods than less active people? Nikki, who's been feeling very hungry and tired after practices, asked Kara if she should eat more. "Training is the only exercise you get," Kara replied. "One hour of real work in a twenty-four-hour day shouldn't take very much food." The answer sounded sensible, and even though Nikki was disappointed, she followed Kara's advice. But Kara was wrong. Since Nikki is exercising, she needs more calories than if she weren't working out. When you exercise, you use up more energy. Your body does need more fuel than less active people.

In fact, you need calories for much more than just your workout. All the things you don't even think about doing require more energy than a one-hour practice! That's because your body's "work" is going on constantly, renewing and replacing your billions of cells, whether you are running, sitting, lying down, or sleeping. And none of that work would get done without the fuel that comes from food. Your most important involuntary muscle, your heart,

A well-balanced diet is essential for an athlete to perform well. Eating foods from the four basic food groups will keep the body running properly.

"works out" every minute of your life. Dozens of muscles contract and stretch so that you blink, yawn, swallow, and digest food—all without remembering to do any of these things! Your intentional motions—reaching, walking, talking, and smiling, to name just a few—require even more of the energy that comes from food.

Stored Energy

When the foods you eat provide less energy (which we measure in calories) than you use in a day, your body doesn't refuse to work. If it did, you'd stop breathing. Instead, it unlocks stored energy deposited throughout your body on the days when

An athlete needs to eat more than less active people because the body needs more energy while exercising.

you ate more calories than you needed. The stored calories are now available from the fat and muscle tissue in your body.

Every body maintains a fat supply as its first source of stored energy. This is the most important of many reasons why some amount of body fat is essential to good health. Your fat also helps maintain a healthy body temperature and cushions your bones. When a girl's or woman's fat supply falls far below healthy levels, her body stops producing estrogen. Menstruation can stop completely.

When there's neither food nor fat to meet the body's constant demands for energy, it still doesn't stop working, though it's tired and weak. To keep going, the body raids its muscle tissues for fuel, breaking them down and converting them back into nutrients to feed itself.

Logically, this muscle loss is the last thing any athlete wants to happen! Your muscle power is the athletic "motor" that you've trained and toned for top performance. Building up major muscle groups is a goal of most athletic training. Greater muscle mass improves your capacity to run, swim, leap, lift, stretch, and power a ball or a bicycle. Well-toned muscles also help deliver the bursts of speed that are critical in many sports. But without regular additions of energy-producing fuel to the body, this "motor" stops working. The smaller, weaker body won't go as far or as fast as it once did.

The "Order" in Eating Disorders

3

Kara, Nikki's track team "buddy," is popular with students and admired by their parents and teachers. She devotes several hours a week to Drama Club and student government in addition to her training and meet schedule, and never seems to run out of energy. Kara's grades are good and she even "has a life," *going to movies and the mall with her friends. Nikki's parents know about Kara's reputation as a school leader and achiever. They're pleased that Nikki got such a fine student as her "buddy," and they think Mr. McCarthy, the coach, must see similar potential in their daughter. But Nikki's parents have never heard about Kara's strict food list or workout requirements for "slipping up" and eating more than she allows. "You should handle this like a pro, on your own," Kara told Nikki when she explained how to keep track of each day's calories.*

Some people don't believe that anorexia nervosa and bulimia nervosa are illnesses because many of the people who suffer from them strive to appear healthy, even "ideal." We're taught to practice self-discipline and to admire the people who show it by getting good grades and becoming better athletes. They hold themselves to high standards and often juggle full schedules. You may measure your own dedication to your sport by noting all the things you give up—parties, television, vacations—to concentrate on it.

Self-Control

Eating disorders are illnesses, not weaknesses. Athletes and other strong, high-achieving people can develop them. (Young anorexia sufferers tend to have better grades and higher ambitions, on average, than their peers who don't have a disorder.) They set personal goals that are admired by teammates, families, and friends. Young male athletes who develop eating disorders often begin by fasting or purging to meet personal or team goals for a specific event. They may be singled out by coaches and sportswriters as role models of dedication for less experienced athletes, as Kara was when she became Nikki's buddy.

Kara's self-control is a positive aspect of her character. Sadly, though, good self-control may actually make it easier for her to develop an eating disorder. This is because she is willing to go hungry without complaining or "giving in" to food. In other words, the very things that make someone a good athlete—discipline, competitiveness, perfectionism—also contribute to eating disorders.

Being in Control

In your pre-teen and teen years, you'll probably become impatient to take control of some aspects of your life as you seek your own identity. Both food and sports can satisfy this need for control and independence. If you're putting in lots of time at the gym, rink, track, barre, or weight room to reach ever higher performance levels, you're probably as tough on yourself as any coach. Meanwhile, your parents continue to expect you at dinnertime, check your homework, or shop for clothes with you.

As control of your life is shifting—usually too slowly for you and too fast for your parents—away from your parents and into your hands, there are many areas of confusion, guesswork, and struggle. You may agree, for example, that you should have a curfew on school nights, but feel that eight PM is too early. Or you may think it's fair that you do some housework, but not the chores your mom wants you to do. But many teens already control when and what they eat without drawing a lot of attention to themselves. They graze from the refrigerator when they please, have money for school lunches and fast food, and eat dinner earlier or later than the rest of the family to go to practices, games, and lessons.

Along with the need to assert control, many teens who develop eating disorders believe that to succeed in life they must change the way they look and reach an ideal set by others. Males and females with these disorders often believe that dieting or purging will help them attain beauty, popularity, or success, because their natural weight and natural eating habits aren't good enough. This attitude of low self-esteem is fed by the ideas that a thin, toned body is ideal and can be created by hard work. Even if you know this is wrong, the message is hard to ignore.

Most girls who stay in competitive sports show higher self-esteem and more self-discipline than classmates who don't commit to practice and improve in sports.

Even so, these girls may believe that their sport requires a very specific ideal body. In this situation, high self-esteem may not be enough to prevent eating disorders. Gina's love of dance is a positive emotion. But she also believes her pride in refusing dinner is positive. Ultimately, both make it easier for her not to eat.

Some athletes develop compulsive food and exercise rituals as a form of self-discipline. These rituals become the goals they can always achieve, unlike the games or races they can't win every time. If they get frustrated with a loss or a bad practice, skipping meals or doubling their workouts is their way of testing their willpower, or punishing themselves for a "failure."

How Do I Know If I Have a Problem?

As you can see, a good character and a strong body cannot protect an athlete from developing an eating disorder. Are you wondering if you have eating habits that could hurt? Answer these questions to help yourself decide. If you answer yes to these questions, please consider getting help.

- ❏ Is the habit a secret? Hiding your food choices, fasting, bingeing, or purging from others is a danger sign for eating disorders. If you think your eating patterns or weight-loss goals are too weird to explain to anyone, they probably are.

If you're afraid to tell someone about them, why?

❑ When someone offers nutrition advice or a food item, what happens? If a simple eating suggestion or the offer of a small treat makes you angry, you may be engaged in an emotional battle with that person. You may be struggling with that person about who is in control of your eating.

❑ Do you buy, cook, or eat food just for yourself? Some athletes do this because they think no one else will understand or accept their food choices. Others are convinced that their special need to become faster, better, and stronger than the competition requires a diet too severe for "ordinary" people, especially the less athletic members of their own families.

❑ Are you afraid that if you stop your food and exercise habits your life will be ruined? Believing that your whole future depends on what you eat is one of the signs of an eating disorder.

Weaker, Slower, Worse: The Real Consequences of Eating Disorders

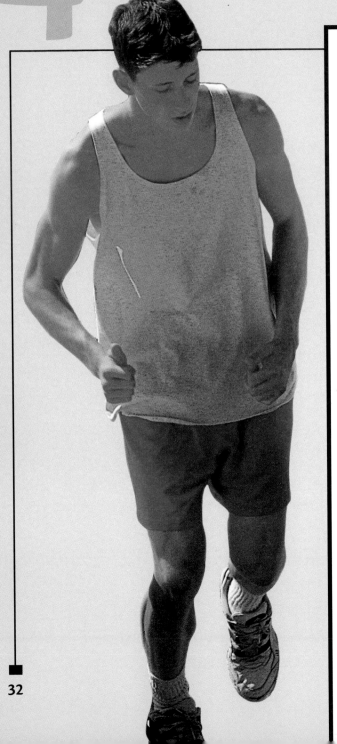

Anorexia and bulimia are dangerous illnesses that afflict hundreds of thousands of women and thousands of men every year. It is estimated that more than 8 million Americans suffer from eating disorders. Anorexia can even be fatal, killing 6 to 18 of every 100 people with this disorder.

Learning the facts about eating disorders will help you realize that no athlete can get faster, stronger, and better at a sport because of an eating disorder.

Anorexia Nervosa

Anorexia nervosa is diagnosed in a person who:

❏ Weighs at least 15 percent less than the

minimum normal weight for her
height, but has no physical illness that
is causing the weight loss,

□ Has an intense fear of becoming fat,

□ "Sees" her body as normal or over-
weight, despite being visibly underweight, and

□ If a girl or woman of menstruating age
has not had a period for at least three
months.

What happens when a body is deprived of 15 percent or more of its minimum proper weight? In a
matter of weeks or months, the person with anorexia experiences one, some, or all of the following
physical problems:

□ Being frequently cold, even in summer
or in well-heated rooms. The body is
burning up its essential fat stores to
meet energy needs because there is no
food in the system. As a result, the
thin layer of subcutaneous (under-the-
skin) fat is vanishing. This is the fat
that helps you maintain normal body
temperature.

❏ Feeling light-headed and dizzy; possibly fainting. An anorexic athlete is depriving the heart, blood, brain, and other systems of vital supplies. Severe dieting means less blood is circulating through the body, causing lower blood pressure and dizzy spells. Starvation also affects the heart muscle. Many anorexics develop a slow or irregular heartbeat.

❏ Becoming more forgetful and having trouble concentrating. A person may feel irritable, unhappy, and pessimistic. These feelings are probably caused by the steady hunger and weakness that result from self-starvation. But they can also be symptoms of depression, a dangerous emotional disorder that can occur whether or not an eating disorder is also present. If you have had these symptoms—changed sleeping patterns, feelings of hopelessness, inability to concentrate or remember things—for two weeks or more, speak to a counselor or call one of the hotlines listed at the back of this book.

Physical Consequences
Menstrual periods stop in a girl or woman who isn't

pregnant when her body-fat stores are too low to support a healthy reproductive system. This is called amenorrhea. Anorexia is one cause of amenorrhea because of drastic weight loss. With treatment, she can begin eating adequately. When her weight and body fat climb back to minimum healthy levels, her periods will start again.

Osteoporosis, which means losing bone mass, is another danger signal, and harder to restore than menstruation. All sports, especially weight lifting and rowing, help to build bone mass, or bone density. Bone mass provides strength and support for all your weight-bearing activities, including "bearing" yourself as you walk, run, stand, or sit. Bone building is a constant process requiring calcium and, in women, estrogen.

How can women athletes work out

Anorexia is characterized by self-starvation. It can cause severe stomach cramps because the body is trying to hold on to any available nutrients.

Osteoporosis, or loss of bone mass, is symptom of eating disorders. Weakened bones, in turn, can be easily injured in high-impact sports.

more than the average person but lose bone mass, when exercise increases bone mass? Health experts believe that when self-starvation becomes so severe that an anorexic woman stops getting her periods, she also produces less estrogen. Without enough estrogen to maintain and increase bone mass, her bones get weaker. They will shrink if the condition is not treated. If a young woman hasn't yet grown to her adult height, osteoporosis can stunt her growth.

Bone density is quickly lost, but slowly restored. If you stayed in bed for just one week with the flu or a broken leg, you'd lose up to 1 percent of your bone mass, and you'd need four months on your feet to get it back. Weakened bones fracture more easily from the unavoidable stresses and impacts of sports: football tackles, gymnastic dismounts, and the pounding that runners absorb with every step.

The most serious complication of anorexia occurs when the body's digestive system simply shuts down and the patient starves to death. This is rare, and so horrifying that many people don't believe it can happen. But the body's ability to process food, like muscle tone and memory, is something you have to use or you'll lose it. People whose anorexia goes untreated also can suffer heart and kidney failure serious enough to kill them.

The Female Athlete Triad

Some athletes think that their good training habits and above-average strength will protect them from the bad effects of chronic undereating. This is not true. In fact, girl and women athletes face an additional risk from untreated eating disorders. This risk is called the female athlete triad, after the three health problems that occur together in many women athletes: disordered eating, loss of menstrual periods, and loss of bone mass.

One of these conditions can signal that the body's essential nutrients and tissues are being "raided," usually by a combination of starvation and overexercising. When all three conditions appear at the same time, it is a health emergency. Experts say that as many as 30 percent of female athletes in sports such as gymnastics, long-distance running, and figure skating suffer from the female athlete triad.

Bulimia Nervosa

A person who suffers from this binge-and-purge disorder faces different, but still damaging, results for her health. Bulimia nervosa is diagnosed in a person who:

- ❑ Overeats in repeated food "binges" for three months or more and feels that she cannot stop eating during a binge,

- ❑ Compensates for binges and tries to avoid gaining weight by vomiting, taking laxatives or other diet drugs, fasting, or excessive exercise, and

- ❑ Ties her self-esteem to her appearance and weight.

Eating disorder experts believe that someone with bulimia can't tell the difference between the sensation

A person with bulimia feels compelled to binge and purge. Bingeing is often triggered by painful emotions, such as anxiety, anger, and fear.

of hunger and such overwhelming emotional sensations as anxiety, embarrassment, and fear. In other words, he or she "feels" nervousness about a final exam, a big swim meet, or a move to a new town as an urge to eat.

A person with bulimia shops or raids the refrigerator for huge amounts of food, much of it snack food or sweets, which is eaten quickly and usually alone. This person then gets the food out of the system after eating by vomiting. People with bulimia learn to provoke vomiting, usually by sticking their fingers far down their throats. They don't do this because they enjoy it. It never feels good. It's messy, foul-smelling, and often painful, but bulimics believe it's absolutely necessary.

People suffering from bulimia also may get rid of the food they consume during binges by taking over-the-counter drugs such as laxatives or diuretics that rush the food through their systems. Athletes may think there's a short-term advantage for losing the "extra baggage" in their stomachs before qualifying weigh-ins or short, intense events like the 50-yard dash, hurdles, and swimming relays, and wrestling matches.

Physical Consequences

By upsetting normal digestive processes, bulimia causes many health problems. A bulimic person's disorder and its complications often go unnoticed because the binges are kept secret. Unlike the person with anorexia who is noticeably "too skinny," the person with bulimia is less likely to be seriously underweight or to stop eating regular meals.

The most obvious symptoms are dry skin, brittle nails, or bleeding gums caused by the lack of vitamins and minerals in the body. Purging rituals get food out of the body before its nutrients can be absorbed. Without these nutrients, the body can suffer from malnutrition even if that person is not too thin and eats regular meals at other times. In addition to tiredness, skin problems, and weak eyesight, vitamin and mineral deficiencies can cause serious unseen harm to the bulimic person's heart, kidneys, and bones.

The teeth develop cavities or "raggedy edges," and the gums may be swollen and tender. This happens because vomiting brings stomach acids up to the mouth. These acids, strong enough to break down foods, are also strong enough to wear away tooth enamel and the softer tissues of the mouth. If a person vomits frequently, he or she is likely to develop tooth decay and gum disease.

A person will have stomach pains. Vomiting is a violent reflex that batters the esophagus and stomach lining. The damage is invisible, but so serious that it can be painful for a person to swallow anything, even water. A person also may have frequent cramps and indigestion. If someone purges frequently with laxatives, he or she may become dependent on them for normal bowel movements.

If you think you may suffer from an eating disorder, it's extremely important to get help. Consider speaking with someone you trust, such as a parent, a friend, or a counselor. You can also contact one of the organizations listed at the end of this book for more information and help. Recovery is a long process, but with help, many people do get better.

"This Isn't an Eating Disorder": The Trouble with Disordered Eating

5

Anorexia and bulimia are serious illnesses that must be diagnosed by doctors, and people who suffer from them need treatment to get better. But athletes who experiment with starving, bingeing, and purging can get hurt, even if they don't have an eating disorder. Their experiments, called disordered eating behaviors, are risky because they can become habits, then uncontrollable urges. Even a single episode, if it is very extreme, can make athletes so tired, thirsty, or dizzy that they get injured or sick. An athlete who can honestly say "I don't have an eating disorder" may still have a troubled relationship with food and body size.

Nikki's health class is in the middle of a unit about eating disorders. One day the teacher introduces a guest speaker, a family therapist for girls and women with eating disorders. Her topic is "Clues that a friend may have anorexia or bulimia."

The therapist asks familiar questions. "Does your friend always bring talk around to the subject of food? This could be a warning. Does she have elaborate cooking or dining rituals? Is she a perfectionist? Does she believe she has to earn everything she eats?" Nikki has seen three different TV movies about anorexia and bulimia, and she's heard all these "clues" before. The one about perfectionism reassures her: I'll never be perfect, she tells herself, so I can't be the eating disorder type.

But Nikki pays attention to the speaker, partly because there's nothing else to do and partly because she wonders if Kara, who is a perfectionist, might have an eating disorder. Is she secretive? She always reminds Nikki not to mention their lists and rules to her parents. Does she have elaborate food rituals? She keeps her lists, but there's no special way that she eats.

Some athletes will exercise compulsively right before a competition in order to meet the weight requirements of a sport such as wrestling.

She does talk about "earning" her calories by working out and improving her personal records, but three other girls on the track team talk the same way, and they're all thinner than Kara.

If Kara had anorexia, Nikki finally decides, she'd look too sick to race. But if Kara's food rules are so smart, why are they both posting slower times than they did at the beginning of the season? What if there's something wrong with Kara? she wonders.

Theo's wrestling team is represented in all weight classes from 106 up to 215. His teammates at the lower weights do not have to watch what they eat at all—in fact, *they can't seem to gain weight even when they try! Theo has never taken a purging drug, but he has skipped meals for up to 24 hours before a weigh-in when he's close to his limit. Some of his teammates in higher weight classes do more than skip meals. They try to sweat off extra pounds by wearing two or three layers of rubber workout suits while they jump rope, punch bags, sprint across the gym, and lift weights. They sweat buckets and get very thirsty, but they won't drink water before a weigh-in. They just rinse and spit so that their mouths won't feel so dry.*

At the seven AM weigh-in, some of the bigger wrestlers are groggy and light-headed. One slips off the scale, stumbles, and lands on his rear end, giggling and shaking his head. But everyone on the team "makes his weight" and the whole team shouts and cheers. Now Theo needs to get his strength up. He's ravenously hungry. To make up for not eating the day before, his backpack is crammed with sandwiches, bananas, and candy bars.

Males and Eating Disorders

Most male athletes never try a slow, gradual weight-loss program because they don't need to lose weight. But they may try to lose or gain pounds quickly for a competitive edge in a big game. Afterward, they'll return to pre-game form in a day or two. Despite this "game day" approach to disordered eating, some boys and men develop anorexia or bulimia. Experts estimate that 1 to 3 of every 100 teen and young adult men, not all of them athletes, will develop an eating disorder at some time. This is only about one-tenth the number of women who will develop an eating disorder.

In sports where weight or body-fat percentage is closely monitored—such as wrestling, swimming, and track—male athletes are more likely to use over-the-counter drugs to drop a few pounds for a day. Boys and men who are willing to manipulate their weight and shape to reach athletic goals are also more likely to abuse drugs such as anabolic steroids, which can speed up the growth of muscle tissue, or so-called fat-burning drugs and food supplements.

Men who suffer from eating disorders will have

The desire to succeed may be so strong for some athletes that they are willing to abuse drugs such as anabolic steroids to gain an edge over the competition.

different role models, performance goals, and body ideals than women, but their physical symptoms (except for amenorrhea), distorted perceptions, and fear of fat are the same. The high-risk sports for men, like those for women, are the ones where appearance is a big factor in success: bodybuilding, figure skating, and gymnastics.

"I don't have an eating disorder, because . . ."

Athletes have many different reasons for saying they don't have eating disorders. Some of them may fear getting kicked off the team. Others will be embarrassed because they think eating disorders are personality flaws, or that no one in their sport ever gets an eating disorder. While there are real differences between them, disordered eating can certainly lead to a serious eating disorder. Recognizing the signs and symptoms of disordered eating early can help prevent the development of eating disorders.

Read the ways athletes finished this sentence, then decide if they are making safe and sensible choices.

"Guys can't get eating disorders." This is what Theo the wrestler told his girlfriend.

She heard his teammates bragging about who sweated out the most pounds, skipped the most meals, or took the most pills before the weigh-in. She wanted Theo to call an eating disorders hotline for advice.

"I never throw up." Gina, the eighth-grade dancer, can say this truthfully. People like her who routinely deny themselves food and control most of their urges to eat usually have nothing to purge.

"I eat three meals a day." Many teenagers with bulimia can say this. Most bulimics don't look like they're starving, so people don't ask them whether they're eating enough. People with anorexia often hide the true extent of their fasting by sitting down to meals with others, taking a bite or two, and pushing food around their plate. They play the social role of an "eater" so well that nobody sees how little they eat.

"I'm getting my periods." If this is true, the athlete does not have full-fledged anorexia. Do you think girls and women should skip as many meals as they want, as long as they're still menstruating?

"I'm supposed to be this thin. Look at my teammates. Look at these pictures of world-class athletes." In any sport, the champion's claim to fame is not being thin—it's the performing speed, style, precision, and energy. No athlete ever won a medal for dieting!

"I'm never very hungry." This is a true statement for many after severe fasting becomes a habit. When the stomach stops expecting to be filled, it does not give the signal we know as hunger.

Reordering Your Feelings About Food and Sports

Gina wishes she did not have to go to her grandmother's for Thanksgiving dinner. She doesn't want one big meal to ruin her three perfect months of skipping dinner, the longest she's ever done anything on her own.

When everyone sat down to dinner, she was nervous, sure that everyone was watching her. Gina *kept up a steady conversation with her grandmother, cutting up food and moving it around her plate while she talked. A few times, her grandmother watched so closely that Gina ate a bite to avoid suspicion.*

While dessert was served, Gina went to the kitchen to to wash dishes. A sharp pain in her gut almost made her drop a plate, but she held her breath and the pain passed. The next pain didn't go away. She crouched down and held her stomach, but it still hurt.

Her grandmother came into the kitchen a minute later and found Gina curled up on the floor, hugging her waist and crying. She was taken to the hospital's emergency room. Gina was terrified. She had no idea what was wrong with her.

Because girls like Gina begin fasting because they think it will improve their bodies, they may not think anything is going wrong until there's an unavoidable sign of trouble. Gina had no permanent injuries, but she was 5'8" and weighed only 99 pounds that day. A week after she was released from the hospital, Gina and her parents made their first visit to a family therapist. Once a week they meet to talk about Gina's love of dance, her fear of food, and her feelings about growing up.

Nikki approached her health teacher a week after the guest speaker came to class and said, "Is it all right if I ask you something privately?

"This may be none of my business," Nikki began. *"But there's this girl I know who might have an eating disorder. I don't want her to get in any trouble if she doesn't, though. I'm just not sure."* Nikki was scared as she rushed through her words. Was it foolish to make a big deal out of Kara's many little rules and habits?

Ms. Ross spoke right away. "Thanks for telling me this, Nikki. I'm really pleased that you're acting on your concern. You must be a good friend. What else can you tell me about this girl?"

Helping a Friend

If you're worried that a friend may have an eating disorder, what can you do? First, remember that eating disorders are illnesses, and you're not a doctor. You can't cure someone's harmful eating behaviors. Second, you want your friend to feel better and eat better, but you can't make her do anything. Here are some dos and don'ts for raising your concerns:

- DO plan this conversation for a quiet time and place. Creating privacy for a serious talk about personal issues shows your respect, and your friend won't feel trapped.

- DO think about what you will say in advance. Have a plan to end the talk if you begin arguing with each other.

While you can't cure a friend's eating problems, you can try to help by voicing your concerns in a private conversation and by encouraging her to seek professional help.

- ❑ DO ask another person who knows your friend and shares your concern to do this with you.

- ❑ DO have an eating disorders hotline number, brochure, or book with you. When the conversation ends, offer to leave it with your friend.

- ❑ DON'T make demands like "Stop doing this to yourself" or "Start eating like a normal person." Eating disorders are illnesses. A person can't stop anorexia or bulimia without treatment, any more than he or she can stop an allergy or a sprained ankle.

- ❑ DON'T tell your friend, "You're not yourself anymore" or "People are talking about you." Even if it's true, it won't help. The purpose of your talk is to help! Your friend will stop listening, and your message will be lost.

- ❑ DON'T bargain: "If you'll stop dieting, I'll stop biting my nails," or "If you don't stop, I can't be your friend." Just state your concern and your wish for your friend to seek help. If he or she refuses, say, "I may talk to you about this another day if I think you're not getting better. I care about you even if you don't agree with what I'm saying." If your friend is already physically ill or has signs of severe depression DON'T wait for a right time to talk. Instead, tell a responsible counselor, nurse, doctor, or coach right away, and ask him or her to help.

Several months later, Gina writes in her diary: *I'm so excited about dancing school this year! I have my regular lessons, plus tap because people with long legs make great tap dancers, plus I'll work with the little kids, helping them hold their positions just right. I remember the assistant from my first year. She was so happy every time I got something right. I'm going to be just like her. I still love the feeling of "getting it right," and that's what I think little kids should like best.*

I still think about looking weird sometimes, but not as much as I used to. I dance because I like to move and it makes me feel good.

Even when eating disorders are identified in a matter of months, as Gina's was, treatment can take months or years. Doctors, therapists, supportive family, and teammates can help athletes learn new ways of thinking and feeling about how they eat, why they perform, and what it means to be healthy.

Your body needs to see you through many more years of satisfying and meaning-filled life. You can't know today what physical stresses will challenge you in the future, but you'll certainly meet many different ones. Your most rewarding feat may be finishing a marathon, competing in a championship event, having a family, campaigning door-to-door for public office, or lugging a cello to concert dates. A few of you may do all these things! Your healthy body and strong self-image are two of the most important allies you'll ever have, and you are the only person who can keep them both on your side.

Glossary

amenorrhea The disppearance of menstrual periods in women who are not pregnant.

carbohydrate An essential nutrient found in sugars, starches, grains, beans, fruits, and vegetables.

dehydration When the body loses water and other fluids it needs.

deprivation The act of withholding something.

diuretic A substance that speeds water's removal from the body, usually by urination.

esophagus The throat.

estrogen Female hormone.

fasting To stop eating food for a period of time.

genetic Relating to your physically inherited characteristics. A gene is the part of each human cell that transmits these characteristics from parents to children.

indigestion Inability to digest food.

laxative A drug that relieves constipation.

malnutrition Bad nutrition.

minerals Elements found in food that help to keep the body healthy and normal.

nutrient Provides nourishment.

nutrition How the body processes food.

perfectionism The belief that anything that isn't perfect is not acceptable.

protein An essential part of our body's cells and a nutrient found in meat, milk, fish, and poultry.

self-discipline Giving oneself strict rules to follow in order to improve.

starvation When suffering from extreme hunger; perish from lack of food.

Where to Go for Help

American College of Sports Medicine
c/o Public Information Office
P. O. Box 1440
Indianapolis, IN 46206-1440
(317) 637-9200

Anorexia Nervosa and Related Eating Disorders, Inc. (ANRED)
P. O. Box 5102
Eugene, OR 97405
(541) 344-1144
Web site: http://www.anred.com

Eating Disorders Awareness and Prevention, Inc. (EDAP)
603 Stewart Street, Suite 803
Seattle, WA 98101
(206) 382-3587
Web site: http://members.aol.com/edapinc

Gürze Books
P.O. Box 2238
Carlsbad, CA 92018-9883
(800) 756-7533
Web site: http://www.gurze.com
Gürze Books is a publisher that focuses on eating disorders. Their books can be ordered directly and will be sent in a plain, confidential package.

National Association of Anorexia Nervosa and Associated Disorders (ANAD)
Box 7
Highland Park, IL 60035
(847) 831-3438
Web site: http://www.members.aol.com/anad20/index.html

National Eating Disorders Organization (NEDO)
6655 South Yale Avenue
Tulsa, OK 74136
(918) 481-4044
Web site: http://www.laureate.com

National Federation of State High School Assocations
P. O. Box 20626
Kansas City, MO 64195-0626
(816) 464-5104

National Mental Health Services Knowledge Exchange Network
(800) 790-2647
Web site: http://www.mentalhealth.org

Something-Fishy Eating Disorders Web Site
http//:www.something-fishy.com/ed.htm

Women's Sports Foundation
Eisenhower Park
East Meadow, NY 11554
(516) 542-4700
Web site: http://www.lifetimetv.com/WoSport

In Canada

Anorexia Nervosa and Associated Disorders (ANAD)
109-2040 West 12th Avenue
Vancouver, BC V6J 2G2
(604) 739-2070

The National Eating Disorders Information Centre
College Wing, 1st Floor, Room 211
200 Elizabeth Street
Toronto, ON M5G 2C4
(416) 340-4156

For Further Reading

Berry, Joy. *Good Answers to Tough Questions About Weight Problems and Eating Disorders.* Chicago: Children's Press, 1990.

Bode, Janet. *Food Fight: A Guide to Eating Disorder for Pre-Teens and their Parents.* New York: Simon and Schuster, 1997.

Brumberg, Joan Jacobs. *The Body Project: An Intimate History of American Girls.* New York: Random House, 1997.

Clarke, Nancy. *Nancy Clarke's Sports Nutrition Guidebook*, 2nd ed. Champaign, Ill.: Human Kinetics, 1997.

Cooke, Kaz. *Real Gorgeous: The Truth About Body and Beauty.* New York: W.W. Norton, 1996.

Crook, Marion. *Looking Good: Teenagers and Eating Disorders,* Toronto: NC Press, Ltd. 1992.

Crutcher, Chris. *Staying Fat for Sarah Byrnes.* New York: Greenwillow Books, 1993. This novel is about a boy trying to please two people, his swimming coach and his best friend, with very different ideas about his "ideal" look and weight.

Kano, Susan. *Making Peace with Food.* New York: HarperCollins, 1989.

Kolodny, Nancy J. *When Food's a Foe: How You Can Confront and Conquer Your Eating Disorder.* New York: Little, Brown and Company, 1992.

Siegel, Michele, Judith Brisman, and Margot Weinshel. *Surviving an Eating Disorder: New Perspectives and Strategies for Family and Friends.* New York: HarperCollins, 1997.

Index

About the Author

Eileen O'Brien is a writer, editor, writing teacher, and sports fan who lives in Baltimore, Maryland.

Design and Layout: Christine Innamorato

Consulting Editor: Michele I. Drohan

Photo Credits

Photo on p. 10 © Michael Tamborrino/FPG International; pp. 12, 53 by Ira Fox; pp. 13, 17, 26 by Skjold Photographs; pp. 18, 22 © Tony Demin/International Stock; p. 20a © Ron Chapple/FPG International; p. 44 by John Novajosky; p. 21 © John Michael/International Stock; p. 24 by John Bentham; p. 32 © Jill Sabella/FPG International; p. 35 by Megan Alderson; p.36 © Vladimir Pcholkin/FPG International; p. 39 by Seth Dinnerman; p. 42 © Jim Cummins/FPG International; p. 46 by Ethan Zindler.